# MY LIFE OF ABSURDITY

## The Autobiography of Chester Himes

### VOLUME II

1976

Doubleday & Company, Inc., Garden City, New York

Congress Cataloging in Publication Data

Himes, Chester B   1909–
The autobiography of Chester Himes.

"The works of Chester Himes":
CONTENTS.–v. 1. The quality of hurt.–v. 2. My
life of absurdity.
1. Himes, Chester B   1909–      –Biography.
2. Novelists, American–20th century–Biography.
I. Title.
PS3515.I713Z5      813'.5'4 [B]
ISBN: 0-385-08909-0
Library of Congress Catalog Card Number: 71-157601

*for my wife,*
LESLEY,
*and our cat,*
DEROS

MY LIFE OF ABSURDITY

*1*

Albert Camus once said that racism is absurd. Racism introduces absurdity into the human condition. Not only does racism express the absurdity of the racists, but it generates absurdity in the victims. And the absurdity of the victims intensifies the absurdity of the racists, ad infinitum. If one lives in a country where racism is held valid and practiced in all ways of life, eventually, no matter whether one is a racist or a victim, one comes to feel the absurdity of life.

Racism generating from whites is first of all absurd. Racism creates absurdity among blacks as a defense mechanism. Absurdity to combat absurdity.

So it was with me. The first time I read the manuscript of my novel *The End of a Primitive*, I knew I had written an absurd book. But it had not been my intention to write about absurdity. I had intended to write about the deadly venom of racial prejudice which kills both racists and their victims. I had not intended to write about absurdity because the book was about me and I had not known at the time that I was absurd.

I thought I had struck a great blow against racial prejudice. I felt like a hero, a warrior in the battle for Negro rights in America. I felt that by writing this book I had won a battle.

I was arrogant in the belief that I had performed a heroic service which made me a hero. I thought I was brave, and that other people were being absurd.

I did not know that the people with whom I came into contact thought I was acting a fool; well not a fool maybe, but presumptuous, audacious. But I felt proud of myself. I felt more like a warrior who has just won a duel. I thought Alva would be proud of me. Women love winners, I thought. I was looking for any sign of racial prejudice to combat it.

Physically I looked like Jesse in *The End of a Primitive*.

I do not know why I did so many things that later seemed absurd. I did not feel absurd. When I discovered that Editions Albin Michel had printed more than ten thousand copies of my book *S'Il Braille Lâche-le*, the French translation of *If He Hollers Let Him Go*, I realized they owed me some money. I don't know why I became upset. It was normal that French publishers never paid black writers all the money their books earned in royalties. Richard Wright had told me the previous year that Albin Michel had paid him an advance for six thousand copies of *Native Son*, which was printed in the same collection, and during the six or seven years since its publication, it had never sold more than six thousand copies. "It's normal, Chester," he had said. I don't know why I became so angry.

I'd heard a number of people in the cafes I went to—the Tournon, Monaco, Petit Suisse—talking about a great new book written by an American *noir*. Marcel Duhamel's translation had become popular in the six years since its publication. William Gardner Smith said he'd heard a great deal of talk about it when he'd been at the writers' colony in La Ciotat the previous summer. But I'd thought nothing of it.

And when I'd talked to an accountant at Editions Albin Michel the day before to get two copies of the book to take to London, she'd said nothing about it other than she had read it and liked it. I had thought they might give me the two copies free, but they only deducted forty per cent of the list price and charged me four hundred francs for the two.

I was in the Café Monaco when I unwrapped them and on the front of the cover of one I saw the figure "10e mille." I knew that was the ten thousandth copy printed. I did a little mental arithmetic and realized if they had sold ten thousand copies they owed me some money. I quickly went to my room and dug up the contract with Albin Michel executed in 1947 and saw they had advanced me one hundred dollars, officially 34,800 francs. At ten per cent of the retail list price, which was my royalty, only one thousand copies should pay me 34,600 francs, and ten thousand copies should pay me 346,000 francs, about a thousand dollars. They owed me about nine hundred dollars. I decided to go back to the firm and find out what was going on.

But I would need someone who spoke fluent French to serve as an interpreter, so I had appealed to Mme. Annie Brière, the journalist who had written an unpublished article about me for the journal France-USA. Mme. Brière wanted to know what was the problem and I had to tell her.

She telephoned the chief accountant for Editions Albin Michel and informed her that I had discovered that ten thousand copies of my book had been printed but I thought I had only been paid the advance for one thousand copies. We were given an appointment for five o'clock that afternoon.

When we arrived the chief accountant presented us with a hastily prepared royalty statement in which I saw many errors in dates alone. Then she went on to say that in 1948 when S'Il Braille Lâche-le was first translated, they had been so enthusiastic they had printed twelve thousand copies as a first printing. (Years later I learned they had printed twenty-four thousand copies—twelve thousand to declare for taxes and twelve thousand to sell under the counter, as was the habit of French publishing houses at that time.) They had distributed these twelve thousand copies in bookstores, she had continued, but ten thousand copies had been returned. So of course they had to sell these as remainders, but I could purchase them myself for cost if I wished. I told her that the day before I had been charged the full list price minus my discount for two copies for my personal use. She blushed slightly and admitted the girl had made a mistake and refunded me my four hundred francs. But I shouldn't be disappointed, she said, for they only owed me 31,650 francs instead of the 300,000 I had thought, and if I would have my agent write them an order they would be happy to pay me this.

Mme. Brière believed implicitly that Editions Albin Michel was honest and that the chief accountant was telling the truth and she seemed upset that I doubted that incredible story. I had been foolish enough to believe she would take my side. I felt affronted. It was all I could do to restrain myself from shouting vile curses and breaking the glass bookcases.

I had already bought my ticket on the boat train to London next morning and had shipped my trunk on ahead, and I restrained myself and resolved to write M. Esménard, the director of Editions Albin Michel. Which I never did. In the meantime that incredible story sat on my stomach like a hard knot.

Editions Albin Michel said they had printed twelve thousand copies of *If He Hollers Let Him Go* but sold only a thousand, which was more or less equal to the advance royalty, whereas they had printed only six thousand copies of *Native Son* in the same collection. My head was throbbing like a mashed thumb when I got to London.

And then one of the most beautiful young women I have ever seen, a mixture of an East Indian mother and a Scottish father, came to my room at ten o'clock that night to measure my foot. I was lying in my bed trying to read and soothe my mind when she walked into my room and looked at me through Scottish blue eyes and said, "May I measure your foot, sir?"

I could just stare at her and giggle uncontrollably. Finally I gasped, "There's nothing wrong with my foot."

"I hope not," she said. "I'm casting a foot for my assignment at school and I need the measurement of an instep." Then I noticed she was wearing a nurse's uniform.

As I look back on my life from the time I sent Alva home, I realize that every moment, every occurrence, every thought, every emotion I experienced was infinitely absurd. Maybe sending Alva home had been absurd. Maybe it was reading my manuscript of *The End of a Primitive* that had made me realize my life was absurd. Given my disposition, my attitude toward authority, my sensitivity toward race, along with my appetites and physical reactions and sex stimulations, my normal life was absurd. I wonder how many people realize their lives are absurd.

Because at that time I did not think my life was absurd; I thought the absurdities came from without, from the people whom I met who were absurd.

I realized, of course, that having my foot measured by the most beautiful girl in the world in the middle of the night was an absurdity not of my making.

And what was more, I was hypersensitive about my feet, especially since I had broken my right toe the year before. They had a tendency toward bunions like my mother's feet, and the toes had been crammed together by wearing shoes too small for me in my youth. I felt about my feet like the eldest of the Karamazov brothers when the police ordered him to take off his shoes and socks; I didn't want anyone to see them and certainly not the most beautiful woman in the world. But she came over and sat on my bed with the greatest of aplomb and reached underneath the covers and drew out my foot and proceeded to measure it. I must have looked like the first black man to see a nude white woman—amazed, embarrassed and hysterical.

When she had finished, she said her name was Simi and thanked me and started to leave. I asked her to stay and have a drink for measuring my foot, but she said the landlord didn't like for her to visit the men's rooms.

I talked to her the next day in the downstairs hall and learned that her mother had been East Indian and her father a Scottish farmer in Kenya, where she had been born and raised, but both her parents were dead and I guessed they lost their lives during the Mau Mau uprising. She was then in London on a fellowship studying chiropody. It seemed the most unlikely pursuit for a young woman with her beauty and sex appeal—she had an unblemished complexion the color of fresh cream, large deep blue eyes, masses of curling black hair and a strong, agile, voluptuous body very adept to fighting off passionate men, I was to learn. For I fell madly in love with her and tried seriously on several occasions to rape her. I suppose she felt sorry for me because I was unsuccessful and black and sick. I suppose all women had felt that way toward me for many years.

I didn't know how sick I was until I received the first stack of letters from Alva, some written on shipboard and others after her arrival in New York. The letters she had written on shipboard were mostly about missing me: "I miss you so much, darling, and I do hope you are very ok there all alone in Paris. Do you get enough to eat? . . ." But the ones she had written after arriving in New York and going about seeing editors crucified me: "Afterwards [after leaving the publishers] I went into the bookshop and looked up Yves' book, it's nicely put out, excellent jacket, linen cover, light gray with blue lettering inside, it's very nice with a good writeup of Yves on the jacket. Also on the very next table was Mr. Himes' *The Third Generation*, it looked very nice and I was proud to say I knew you and Yves. Richard Wright's *Black Power* was there, too, also Billy Smith's *South Street*. I asked about sales, Yves' book fair, that Frank Yerby was the most popular of the colored writers. . . ." I'd feel my brain lurch. *What motherfucking color are writers supposed to be?*

Then it continued: "There are signs in all the subway trains: *To win we need them all, Catholics, Protestants, Jews, Americans of every race, creed and national origin. Fight racial and religious hate.*" And finally: "The lady in the bookshop said she didn't blame Wright for living abroad. I didn't quite get what she meant, but she'd read *Lonely Crusade* and thought it was excellent. . . ."

Ofttimes Simi would visit me during the day against the landlord's wishes. She knew there was something troubling me and tried to help. She wormed out the story of me and Alva. She asked me if the people in the United States would accept us. I told her I'd hate to try. She said in some ways she was in the same predicament. Many rich Indians both old and young were madly in love with her, but none could marry her because of their religion, they could only keep her as a mistress and she didn't want that. She had loved her Scottish father but his blood was the tragedy of her life. I said I'd gladly marry her. She smiled. We got along wonderfully and she cheered me up tremendously. One corner of my room was curtained off for a kitchen and I used to buy streaky bacon, eggs, sugar, tea and bread and prepare my own lunch, making my tea strong enough to float an egg. Sometimes she'd have lunch with me. I invariably tried to seduce her but she was too strong physically. Our landlord and his family could hear us scuffling in the kitchen below, but they never interfered. Her father's family had been acquainted with his family and they thought the world of her. They knew she was engaged mostly in social work with me.

Everyone knew when I got a letter like this from Alva:

"You know, during that weekend in New York alone I understood so much about *The End of a Primitive.* It's a beautiful book, darling, and I love you so very, very much, darling. It was that way from the very first meeting on the ship when I bumped into you. I wouldn't have believed it could happen to anyone ever like that if it hadn't been me. There must be some reason for it, there always is for everything in life. Last year was very hard for you, I know. I hope with all my heart that next year is kinder. Anyway I pray for you, darling, every night, if it helps you to know. And all of my love, darling, for always."

That was when I would begin to cry. I didn't want to cry. But I couldn't help it. Because I knew that America would kill it.

It was like it had been at Yaddo, like I had written in my short story "Da Da Dee": "It was not really crying and not really a song but a series of sounds. It was like human howling. It was melodic in a sense, such as certain phrases of symphonies are melodic. Its underlying melody was that of a popular song called 'I'll Get By As Long As I Have You.' But I didn't know this. . . ."

Those loud weird sounds shattering the quiet night of that sedate rooming house startled the living hell out of the occupants. But only Simi came rushing up to help.

I would be startled out of my wits. I hadn't realized I was making sounds. Once the landlord became so frightened he telephoned for the police. He had a wife and a teen-age daughter. Simi was still in the room when two officers in plain clothes arrived. We could hear the landlord and his wife whispering tensely to the police in the downstairs hallway. Then the landlord came up and asked Simi to come out, and I could hear more whispering. I opened the door onto the landing and looked down and saw five of them huddled in the lower hall. One of the officers looked up and our gazes met; then I closed the door and went to bed. I expected them to come up any minute and ask me to dress and take me to the station, but only Simi came back to tell me the officers had left but if I made any more disturbances they would come back and lock me up.

I smiled and said, "You're too good to me. I'm just a no-good bum."

She touched my cheek gently. "No, you're not; you're sick. Who's been hurting you?"

And it was all I could do to keep from crying again.

After that I tried to keep out of everyone's sight. The young maid who cleaned my room literally trembled in terror at the sight of me. Somehow the landlord and I kept out of each other's way, but on occasion when I saw his wife I would catch a look of infinite pity in her eyes.

I tried to take myself in hand. I went out more, to the movies, for long walks on the Heath or wandered about late at night in Soho and the Piccadilly Circus area.

I visited George Padmore, the Marxist essayist and historian of Africa who had got Richard Wright permission from the Home Office to visit Ghana. His flat was on Baker Street but his wife, Dorothy, was out of town, and it was cold and dark and dreary and when he lit the grate in the sitting room it smelled strongly of gas. We talked mostly of Richard Wright's book *Black Power*, which had resulted from his visit to Ghana. Personally he thought it was a good job and typical of Dick, but he didn't think most Africans would like it. Dick's criticisms were valid enough from an American point of view, but African thinking was different, he said. I thought he was trying to express his opinion in simple terms that I would understand.

Finally I got tired of his defending Dick and his book to me, and told him I not only hadn't read it but I hadn't seen a copy of it. If I had had any opinion at all, even without reading the book, I would have felt Dick was making a mistake. In trying to effect his departure from America and its way of life, Dick had become more of an American than he had ever been. But, whereas in the U.S. he could not escape his image of a *Black Boy*, in Paris he was a rich man. And he enjoyed being a rich man, he loved the bourgeois life. But he wasn't adapted to the bourgeois life. From beginning to end, deep in his soul, Dick identified with the poor and the oppressed. He was a natural-born leftist; and what the French intellectual "left" never forgave him for was not leaving the Communist party, but stoning it after he had left it in his contribution to *The God That Failed*.

"Perhaps you're right," George began, but I wouldn't let him continue.

The French leftist intellectual knew that Dick needed authority; he was rootless without an absolute. And there were only two absolutes open to him in the western civilization—Marxism or Catholicism. He needed one or the other from which to launch his defense of the poor and the oppressed with which he identified. But, eventually, he attacked them both.

George said, "I must go now, Chester, but I would like to talk this out with you sometime."

I don't remember how I spent Christmas 1954 or with whom. I received letters addressed to "Señor Chester Himes y Señora" and "Bien chères Amis" from the friends Alva and I had made in Deyá, thanking us for the presents we had sent for their babies' baptisms. I remembered then that Alva had bought and mailed the presents in Paris before she went back to the U.S., but I had so completely left Mallorca in both body and soul it might have been on the moon.

Judging from her letters, Alva seemed to be incessantly typing copies of *The Golden Chalice*, our autobiography, and corresponding with publishers, worrying about the effect of Dexamyl on my health (the house doctor at the Hotel Tudor in New York had told her that it was especially injurious to the heart and kidneys and over a period of time it would kill you), and worrying about the attitudes of her aunt and uncle in Philadelphia. ("They're very good to me, darling, but they're both very old and a little childish, you know. My Uncle's declined terribly since his shock. He has to be in bed at eight and he can't lift things, and he only goes to work occasionally from nine to four. He has to be very careful. My aunt has slowed up too. . . . They're very good to me, but I have to be very careful of what I say and do. . . .")

She had got a job as a receptionist to a doctor in Philadelphia which paid forty-eight dollars for four eight-hour days a week. She was working herself to the bone, literally, trying to make enough to take care of the expenses of trying to sell the book, and worrying herself sick about me and my health and my finances; and predictably, I got sick and tired of her taking so much upon herself when someone had to do it, sick and tired of her trying so goddamn hard to help me when I needed help so badly, sick and tired of her being so mother-raping good when I was such a heel, and I decided to end it, to finish it off once and for all so I wouldn't have to think of her again and worry because I loved her and get my goddamned self hurt by the way the world accepted her and rejected me. Sick and tired of all the shit that went along with a black man writing.

So I sat down and wrote her this mean and vicious letter, all the while thinking of the Ink Spots rendition of "You Always Hurt the One You Love." And crying way down in the bottom of my heart. But I would write it again under the same circumstances.

*Dear Alva,*

*I have ordered the last of my money from Tangier and when it arrives I shall book passage to New York on the first ship available. I should sail sometime before January 15, and I will write again and let you know the date of my arrival.*

*In the meantime we will plan to submit and publish TGC under both our names. There should be no guilt or shame on either side, since that is the way we wrote it; and if this act of collaboration on a work of art by the two of us does not meet with the approval of sundry persons in our native land, so be it.*

*On re-reading your letters I see again the terrifying destructiveness of American life. Everything seems to go—integrity, self-confidence, honor, trust, gratitude, all human values—with awesome swiftness in the struggle for the dollar. And once gone what have you? What do you really have? A few furs, a few dollars, sleeping around, unhappiness, self-contempt, the flattery of the unimportant. An atrophied brain.*

*I seemed to have been suffering the delusion that you regained a certain faith and perhaps learned a more honest evaluation of life. Anyway, I pray to God that you retain what is good and noble within you—for your own sake. Our living together might have been wrong, but it was not sin, because we brought it so much good that it could never be called sin. The sin would be to let the cheap shabby sacrilegious forces of a greedy and intemperate society buy that which was good on the prostitution market. As far as TGC is concerned, why do it anyway? What would you prove? and to whom? and for what? One must love in this world whom one will. But for what earthly reason should I contribute to your love for your people who drench themselves in self-indulgences (furs, diamonds, waste, etc.) knowing that you, who love them, are sweating out an existence on (as far as they know or care) the charity of a stranger. It doesn't make sense. In fact, I feel that I have opened the wrong door.*

*So I am backing out quietly (as quietly as you will let me) and closing the door gently so as not to disturb anyone. You have impressed me that beyond all doubt that it is your life, I can not live it for you.*

*If you wish, you may continue negotiations on the book with Doubleday and Scribners, and Macmillan (if you have sent them a copy). Philadelphia publishers are out. I will not let the book be published by any one of them. That is to say, continue negotiations in both our names, informing the editors that it is a joint property. If any of them are interested, it would be better to await my arrival and we will go in together. If together you and I should be as successful with this book as "Colored writer" Frank Yerby was with his first book, it will exceed our most optimistic expectations. In any event, as I have told you many, many times, the money is not important. We will sell this book together then you will be completely free to go on with your life in whatever way you see fit.*

I was filled with all manner of suspicions, doubts, antagonisms and resentments because she had returned into her white world, even